春潮NOV+

我 数 到 三 ……

汉 英 对 照

LOVE POEMS

{ for people with children}

［美］约翰·肯尼（John Kenney）/ 著　潘采夫 / 译

中信出版集团 | 北京

图书在版编目（CIP）数据

我数到三……：汉英对照 /（美）约翰·肯尼著；
潘采夫译. -- 北京：中信出版社，2020.10
书名原文：Love Poems for People with Children
ISBN 978-7-5217-2000-6

Ⅰ. ①我… Ⅱ. ①约… ②潘… Ⅲ. ①英语—汉语—
对照读物②诗集—美国—现代 Ⅳ. ①H319.4：I

中国版本图书馆CIP数据核字(2020)第112986号

我数到三……（汉英对照）

著　　者：［美］约翰·肯尼
译　　者：潘采夫
出版发行：中信出版集团股份有限公司
　　　　　（北京市朝阳区惠新东街甲4号富盛大厦2座　邮编　100029）
承　印　者：北京通州皇家印刷厂

开　　本：787mm×1092mm　1/32　　印　张：6.25　　字　数：20千字
版　　次：2020年10月第1版　　　　印　次：2020年10月第1次印刷
京权图字：01-2020-4306
书　　号：ISBN 978-7-5217-2000-6
定　　价：39.80元

献给露露和休伊特，
可能时机不对，不过我想告诉你们
我不是你们真正的父亲。

To Lulu & Hewitt.

Now is probably the wrong time to let you know

that I am not your real father.

要 么 再 给 我 来 点 儿 酒 ， 要 么 让 我 一 个 人 待 着 。

——鲁米（诗人，四个孩子的父亲）

Either give me more wine or leave me alone.

— Rumi (poet, father of four)

我六岁的孩子拿着我的手机

抱歉，牧师：
我六岁的孩子
抓住了
我的手机，
发给了您
一百四十二个
便便表情。

您要知道
那绝对不代表
我对您的看法，
或对教堂有什么意见。
（尽管这确实使我怀疑神的存在。）

致我的岳父，卢：
任何一位外祖父都不应收到
法比奥不穿裤子的动图，
他意味深长地跳着舞，
还招呼着，

"让我们尽情欢乐吧[1]！"
我发誓我已经把它删了。

致我的老板，加里：
您是否不巧收到了一张
狒狒屁股的图片，
下面写着
"发现一张你的照片"？
那是我发的。

1　原文的"get it on"有性交、勃起等意。（本书注释如无特别说
　　明，均为译者注。）

My six-year-old got hold of my phone

My apologies, Reverend.
My six-year-old
got hold
of my phone
and sent you
142
poop emojis.

Please know
that this in no way
reflects my opinion of you
or the Church.
(Although it does make me wonder if there is a god.)

To my father-in-law, Lou.
No grandparent should ever receive
a GIF of Fabio not wearing pants
dancing suggestively
with the words

Let's get it on!
I was sure I had deleted that.

To my boss, Gary.
Did you happen to receive a photo
of a baboon's ass
with a note reading
Found this picture of you?
I sent that one.

如果生孩子也要面试

面试官可能会说，

据说您想要孩子。

您可能会说，是的！我准备好了。

太好了。您的婚姻幸福吗？

非常幸福，我太太非常棒。

很好。我还需要问几个问题。您最后一次参加现场音乐

会是什么时候？

两周前，临时决定的。是一支爵士乐队。

上次乘飞机呢？

在巴黎，我想。是的，我们去巴黎待了四天。

您在飞机上睡觉了吗？

睡了，那是一趟红眼航班。

有人在任何时间吐到您身上了吗？

没有，当然没有。为什么这么问？

有人突然冲着您尖叫把您吵醒了吗？

什么？没有。

我可以问一下您性生活的频率吗？

平均下来，我猜，每周五到六次。

多么美妙。请您从我这里拿走这张纸。您有什么感觉吗?

见鬼……这是什么鬼东西? 黏糊糊又难闻。

您喜欢那种感觉吗?

不!

别大惊小怪,我现在要把这一大杯橙汁倒在您裤腿上。

上帝啊! 简直不敢相信你是来真的。

我要对着您的耳朵发出很响亮的、令人讨厌的声音。告诉我您是不是喜欢。啊啊啊啊啊啊啊 !!!!

你到底有什么毛病,老兄 ?!!

辛普森先生,我有个坏消息要告诉您。

If there were a job interview to have children

The interviewer might say

I see here that you want children.

And you might say, Yes! I'm ready.

Great. Are you happy in your marriage?

Very. My wife is amazing.

Good for you. Just a couple of questions. When's the last time you went to hear live music?

Two weeks ago. Last-minute thing. Saw a jazz band.

Last time on a plane?

Paris, I think. Yes. We went to Paris for four days.

Did you sleep on the plane?

Yes. It was an overnight flight.

Did anyone throw up on you at any time?

No. Of course not. Why?

Did anyone on the plane wake you suddenly by screaming in your face?

What? No.

May I ask about the frequency of your sex life?

Average, I guess. Five or six times a week.

How wonderful. I'd like you to take this paper from me. Do you feel anything?

What the hell . . . what is this? It's sticky and it smells.

Do you like that feeling?

No!

Don't be alarmed but I am now going to pour this large glass of orange juice on your pant leg.

Jesus Christ! I can't believe you just did that.

I'm going to make a very loud, annoying noise in your ear. Tell me if you enjoy it. Ahhhhhhh!!!!

What the hell is wrong with you, man?!!

Mister Simpson, I have some bad news for you.

谁是那个先起床的人

凌晨三点四十二分，宝宝哭了。
又哭了。
谁起床呢？

我知道你
知道我
没有睡着。
我只是在装睡。

但我也知道
你知道
我知道
你在装睡。

因为像我一样，
在装睡这件事上，
你绝对可以获得
奥斯卡金像奖提名。

谁来打破这个僵局?

你说,
如果你起床,我会给你看咪咪。

成交。

Who will be the first to get up?

3:42 A.M. and the baby is crying.
Again.
Who will get up first?

I know that you
know that I
am not asleep.
I'm just faking.

But I also know
that you know
that I know
that you are faking.

Because like me
you have developed the qualities
of an Academy Award–nominated
fake sleeper.

Who will break?

And then you say
If you get up, I'll show you my boobs.

Done.

安静的时光

时间晚了，光线暗了。
故事读完了，该上床睡觉了。

爸爸，你嘟囔着，相扑选手为什么要戴尿布？
没人知道，小伙子。嘘。
皇帝（emperor）为什么站在接球手后面？
是裁判（umpire），小伙子，不是皇帝。嘘。
喊"狼来了"的男孩后来怎么样了？
他长大了，在卖房子。快睡觉。

终于睡着了。
对我来说
很短暂。
我突然清醒，
像猫一样轻手轻脚
朝门进发。
可以喝上一杯啦。

爸爸？

（可恶！该死！小浑蛋！）

怎么了，小伙子？

在《摇一摇，小宝贝》中，为什么宝宝要坐在树顶上？

因为他不去睡觉。

那个宝宝从树上掉下来了吗？

是的，他掉下来了。

摇篮也掉下来了吗？

所有东西都掉下来了，摔得稀巴烂。我不骗你，很糟糕。

那我们为什么要唱它呢？

因为它给我们上了重要的一课。

什么？

保持安静，否则我们会把你放到树上。嘘。

Quiet time

Late now and light low.
Stories read, time for bed.

Dad, you whisper, *why do sumo wrestlers wear diapers?*
No one knows, buddy. Shhh.
Why does the emperor stand behind the catcher?
Umpire, pal. Not emperor. Shhh.
What happened to the boy who cried wolf?
He grew up and works in real estate. Go to sleep.

Sleep finally comes.
For me
briefly.
I wake with a start
move like a cat
head to the door.
Wine time.

Dad?

(Shit! Dammit! Little bastard!)

Yes, buddy?

In "Rock-a-bye Baby," why is the baby on top of a tree?

Because he wouldn't go to sleep.

The baby fell out of the tree?

He did, yes.

And the cradle fell, too?

The whole thing. Crashed to the ground. I won't lie,
    it was bad.

Why do we sing that?

Because it teaches us an important lesson.

What's the lesson?

Be quiet or we put you in a tree. Shhh.

我哺乳期的乳房

我知道在你看来，
把我的
乳房紧紧挤压，
就像打开杂货包装袋，
对我来说
似乎很有趣。
然而，并不是。

我不觉得这性感。
它们很痛，
而且充满了
给我们宝宝的奶水。

还有，
"看看这两个'大奶罐'"
不是我现在（以及任何时候）
想听你说的话。

我还要补充一点，

你的确可以在某些时候和场合
触摸它们，
但并不是
上周为你叔叔守灵的时候。

如果我
走到你面前
捏着你的小弟弟，你会怎么想？

哦。那不是我想要的回答。

My breast-feeding breasts

I know that to you
it might seem like it
would be fun for me
to have my
boobs squeezed
as I unpack the groceries.
It's not, though.

I'm not feeling sexy.
And they're sore
and full of milk
for our baby.

Also
Look at those jugs
is not what I want to hear
from you right now. (Ever?)

And may I add

that there is a time
and a place to touch them.
And that time was not
at your uncle's wake last week.

What if I
just walked up to you
and squeezed your penis?

Oh. That was not the answer I was expecting.

我们现在不可能做爱了，是吗

你上床睡觉时
脸上有一种表情。
好吧，我不能完全看清你的脸，
所以只是推测你脸上有一种表情。
因为你有一段时间没看我了，
从我们争吵之后。

显然，凡事要从两面看。
好吧，也许这件事只有一面，
而你是对的。

也许我至今还没有道歉
是因为我的情商
只有一罐肉汁那么多。
（这是你的话，但没错。）

但是现在你穿着
内裤和一件 T 恤。

虽然看不到你的脸，
但可以看到你的屁股，
真的很有魅力。

我觉得能看见你的屁股，
就是你在向我传达信号：
一切已经过去了，
而你想做爱。

但事实证明这根本不是什么信号。
只是我能看见而已。

"我有没有说过我很抱歉？"我边说
边试图触摸你没有传达任何信号的屁股。

想都别想，你说，
打开了我的手。

很好。
信号收到了。

There isn't a chance in hell we're having sex now, is there?

You have a look on your face
as you get into bed.
Well, I assume you have a look on your face
as I can't quite see your face
because you haven't looked at me for a while.
Ever since we argued.

There were two sides, of course.
Fine. Maybe just the one side.
And maybe I wasn't on it.

And maybe I haven't apologized yet
because I have the emotional intelligence
of a can of gravy.
(Your words, but not wrong.)

But now you are in your
underwear and a T-shirt.

And while I can't see your face
I can see your butt
which looks very nice to me.

I assume that my ability to see your butt
is a signal from you to me
that all is forgiven
and that you want to have sex.

But it turns out it's not a signal at all.
It's just my ability to see.

Did I mention I'm sorry? I say
attempting to touch your non-signaling butt.

Don't even, you say
swatting my hand away.

Very good then.
Signal received.

分娩痛

打完无痛分娩针后，
你设法在产房里
小憩。

我看着你，
我可爱的妻子，
想着孩子时我满面笑容，
但也有点儿饿。

你有没有打包一个三明治或其他吃的？
我小声问你。
见你没有回应，
我摇了一下你的手臂。

所以这就是我接下来所做的事 ——
我不想再打扰你了 ——
我穿过马路，
买了一个速食汉堡和一杯啤酒。
我决定在酒吧坐坐，

因为我也有点儿累。
也许我只是饿了，
那个汉堡美味极了。

于是我又来了一杯，
并开始和酒保聊天。
他就是那个
在搞清楚状况后
建议我也许应该回到医院的人。
（是个好人。）

尽管当我们的儿子出生时，
严格来说我并没有和你一起待在产房里，
但我的心确实在那儿。

我们应该改天再去一次那家酒吧。

Labor pain

After the epidural
you managed to nap
in the delivery room.

And I watched you
my lovely wife
smiling at the thought of our child
but also a little hungry.

Did you pack a sandwich or anything?
I whispered to you
shaking your arm a bit
when you didn't respond.

So what I did was—
because I didn't want to bother you anymore—
I went across the street
to grab a quick burger and a beer.

I decided to sit at the bar
because I was kind of tired too.
Maybe I was just hungry
but it was a really good burger.

So then I had a second beer
and got to chatting with the bartender.
He was the one who suggested
that maybe I should get back to the hospital
when he found out what was going on.
(Great guy.)

And while I wasn't technically in the room with you
when our son was born
I was certainly there in spirit.

We should all go back to that bar sometime.

我数到三

我是认真的，小姐，

你不会希望我数到三的。

一……

二……

该死。

她一动不动。

一个人在数到三之后要做什么？

数到四吗？

有没有人数到过四？

数到四之后又该怎么办？

数到五？

数到十？

数到一百会怎样？

那时的惩罚该有多重？

送进科罗拉多州的超级监狱？

我要给你第二次机会。

按照我的要求去做，把你的东西收拾好。

不。

收好你的背包。

不。

整理好蜡笔？

不。

你愿意做什么？

看《小医师大玩偶》？

成交。

I am going to count to three

I mean it, young lady.
You do NOT want me to count to three.
1 . . .
2 . . .

Dammit.
She's not budging.
What does one do after three?
Go to four?
Has anyone ever gone to four?
What is the protocol on four?
Is it possible to go to five?
To ten?
What happens at 100?
What's the punishment there?
A supermax prison in Colorado?

I'm going to give you a second chance.
Do what I asked and put your things away.

No.

Put your backpack away.

No.

Clean up your crayons?

No.

What are you willing to do?

Watch *Doc McStuffins*?

Deal.

请尊重我的隐私

我坐在马桶上，
门开着。

你在那里站着，
你就快两岁了。

嗨，爸爸！
你说。

嗨，亲爱的，
我回应。

你要去洗手间吗？
你问。
当然了，我说。

但是我需要一点儿隐私，
请关上门。
你关上了，

从里面。

所以，爸爸，你问，
我们要聊些什么？

Privacy please

As I sit on the toilet
the door opens.

There you stand
almost two years old.

Hi Dad!
you say.

Hi sweetie
I respond.

Are you going to the bathroom?
you ask.
Sure am, I say.

But I need some privacy.
Close the door please.
And you do.

From the inside.

So, Dad, you ask.
What should we talk about?

我知道，巴士的轮子会一直转啊转

我知道。
我了解轮子、喇叭和婴儿。
每个人都了解。

不过有些事情你可能不了解。
这辆巴士上的爸爸在想，
这不是我上车的目的。
也许巴士的驾驶员
也在想着完全相同的事情。

也许司机回头看着爸爸，
却没有催他往后走。
也许他反而点头微笑，
爸爸也点头微笑。
司机猛踩油门，
嗡，嗡，嗡，
速度太快以至于巴士上的妈妈们都嚷起来：
万能的主啊，开慢点！
司机在街道拐角处嘎的一声停下来，

因为他看到一家"早上九点营业"的酒吧。
他和爸爸下车走进了酒吧。

叫一辆优步吧，
因为此巴士已停用。

唱那首诗吧，为什么不呢？

I am fully aware that the wheels on the bus go round and round

I get it.
I know about the wheels and the horn and the babies.
Everyone knows that.

Here's something you might not know.
The daddy on *this* bus is thinking
This is not what I signed up for.
And maybe the driver on the bus
is thinking the exact same thing.

Maybe he looks over at the daddy
and he doesn't go *Move on back.*
Maybe instead he nods and smiles.
And the daddy nods and smiles.
And the driver hits the gas
and goes zoom, zoom, zoom
so fast that the mommies on the bus say
Jesus Christ almighty, slow down!

And the driver screeches to a halt at the corner
because he sees a sign for a bar called "Open at 9 A.M."
and he and the daddy get off the bus and go into the bar.

Call an Uber
because this bus is out of service.

Sing *that* verse, why don't you.

谈话

好了，儿子。
我们在
开车
去开市客超市的路上，
去买五十盒一包纸巾。

你现在十岁了，
哇。
我十一岁了，爸爸，你说，
我们为什么要走这么远？
还有你为什么要抽烟？

问得好，
但我要问你一个问题。
你知道你的小弟弟，对吗？

等等，什么？
你问，盯着我。

儿子，假设一个男人有一个小弟弟，那个小弟弟……

爸爸，这是数学题吗？

像是：假设一辆火车在早上九点离开芝加哥……

不，不是数学问题，

这是小弟弟问题。

好吧，本质上不是个问题。

你看，一个女人有一个阴道，

而小弟弟和阴道打招呼。

哈！小弟弟会说话！

格伦在学校用他的午餐盒跟女生搭讪。

不要想格伦了。

当一个男人和一个女人彼此相爱时……

你和妈妈要离婚吗?!

不，不，天哪，不是，你妈妈非常喜欢我。

不，我是在谈论有关……嗯……

做爱。

性交……

哦。格伦说首先你需要勃起。

好吧，格伦对极了。
想想看，
也许你只需要和格伦谈谈。

The talk

Well, son.
Here we are
in the car
driving to Costco
for a fifty-pack of paper towels.

You're ten years old now.
Wow.
I'm eleven, Dad, you say.
Why are we going the long way?
And why are you smoking?

Great questions.
But here's a question for you.
You know your penis, right?

Wait. What?
you ask, staring at me.

Son, let's say a man has a penis and that penis . . .

Dad. Is this a math problem?

Like: if a train leaves Chicago at nine A.M. . . .

Nope. Not a math problem.

It's a penis problem.

Well, not a problem per se.

You see, a woman has a vagina.

And the penis and vagina say hello.

Ha! A talking penis!

Glen at school does a talking penis thing with his lunch box.

Forget Glen for a minute.

When a man and a woman love each other . . .

Are you and Mom getting a divorce?!

No no. God no. Your mother likes me very much.

No, I'm talking here about . . . well . . .

Lovemaking.

Intercourse . . .

Oh. Glen says you need a boner first.

Well, Glen is spot-on there.
Come to think of it
maybe just talk to Glen.

班尼¹死了，甜心

我知道这很让人伤心。
他怎么死的？
嗯，班尼很老了。
你知道恐龙是如何灭绝的吗？
灭绝意味着你不应该再活着。
这只是一个粗略的解释，
当然。
无论如何，他是最后一只恐龙，
现在，他走了。

还有一件关于卡由的趣事。
他去度假了，
永远。
你记得我们如何
在祖母那里度假，
度过了那痛苦的一周吗？
我的意思是美好的一周？
嗯，就像那样，
除了食物可能好一点儿。

哦，我最近在新闻中看到

汪汪队去执行了最后一次任务。

显然他们退休了。

然后泡泡孔雀鱼搬到了凤凰城²。

还有朵拉……可怜的朵拉在探险中走得有点儿太远了。

看，亲爱的，《谍影重重》开始了。

你会喜欢的。

1 班尼：美国动画片《紫色小恐龙班尼》的主人公，下文中提到的卡
   由、汪汪队、泡泡孔雀鱼、朵拉都是美国动画片中的角色。

2 凤凰城是美国养老胜地。

Barney died, sweetheart

It's sad, I know.
How did he die?
Well, Barney was old.
And you know how dinosaurs are extinct?
Extinct means you no longer deserve to live.
That's just a rough definition
of course.
Anyway he was the last dinosaur.
And now he's gone.

And here's a funny story about Caillou.
He went on vacation.
Forever.
You know how we go on vacation
to your grandmother's
for one agonizing week?
I mean wonderful week?
Well, it's like that.
Only the food is probably better.

Oh. And I saw on the news recently that

Paw Patrol went on their last mission.

Apparently they retired.

And the Bubble Guppies moved to Phoenix.

And Dora . . . poor Dora went a little too far exploring.

Look, sweetheart. *The Bourne Identity* is on.

You'll like this.

你所说的性爱时间，
我称之为想事情的最好时机

感觉好吗？你问。

我很愉快，我答道，注意力有点儿分散，

立即后悔用了"愉快"一词。

愉快？你说，困惑又受伤。

对不起，我的意思是非常棒。

你在想什么？你问，试图表现得很性感。

你，我说谎，

当然是你，还有……很多……性感的东西……

比如说我们该买牛奶了，

还有卫生纸，

还瞥了一眼窗户，

注意到它们需要清洗，

以及我忘了给姐姐回电话。

哦，还有我的鞋子在修鞋匠那里。

"修鞋匠"是个有趣的词。

修鞋匠。

我大声说出了"修鞋匠"。

你说：

哦是啊，你是我肮脏的桃红色小修鞋匠，不是吗？

当然，随你怎么说。

我不是，

但是谢谢你提醒我，

我需要去农贸市场买桃子。

What you call sex I call a wonderful time to make a mental list

Is this good? you ask.

It's very pleasant, I respond, distracted,

immediately regretting the word "pleasant."

Pleasant? you say, confused and hurt.

Sorry, I meant amazing.

What are you thinking about? you ask, trying to be sexy.

You, I lie.

Of course you. And . . . lots of . . . sexy things . . .

Like the fact that we need milk.

And paper towels.

And glancing over at the windows

I notice that they need to be washed.

And I forgot to call my sister back.

Oh, and my shoes at the cobbler.

"Cobbler" is a funny word.

Cobbler.

Except I say cobbler out loud.

And you say

Oh yeah. You're my dirty little peach cobbler, aren't you?

Sure, whatever.

I'm not.

But thank you for reminding me

that I need to go to the farmer's market.

婴儿湿巾

如果你
在我二十多岁时告诉我，
我会做这样的事，
我不会相信。

但是今天早上，
婴儿的便便
像炮弹一样射出来，
其中一些落在了我的头发上。

好吧，我很累，
而且我想我太懒了，
不想洗澡。
再说我上班要迟到了。

所以我
扯出一张婴儿湿巾，
把便便从头发上擦去。

不管怎样，把大部分擦去了。

然后继续我的一天。

Baby wipes

If you had told me
in my twenties
that I would do this,
I wouldn't believe you.

But this morning,
the baby's poop
shot out like a cannonball
and some of it landed in my hair.

Well, I was pretty tired
and I guess too lazy
to shower.
And I was late for work.

So what I did
was take a baby wipe
and clean it out of my hair.

Most of it, anyway.

Then I went on with my day.

家庭假期

在我们假期的
第一天，
我躲在
十分拥堵的 95 号州际公路旁
一个休息站中
罗伊·罗杰斯快餐店的
男厕里，
心想，
这才叫放松。
与此同时孩子们
在车后座
用网球拍
继续打斗。
只要再开五个小时就到了。
"我不想离开这地方。"
我忍不住响亮地说出来。
"我也不想。"
旁边隔间的那个男人说。

Family vacation

This *is* relaxing
I think to myself
on the first day
of our vacation
as I hide
in the men's room
of a Roy Rogers
at a rest stop
just off bumper-to-bumper I-95
while the kids
continue fighting
with tennis racquets
in the back seat.
And only five more hours to go.
I don't want to leave this place
I whisper aloud.
Neither do I
says the man in the next stall.

解析你的学前班艺术作品

我为你做了这个，妈妈！

亲爱的，这……真是……太——棒——了。

但是你根本没看。你在看手机。

对不起，宝贝。我现在看到了。

猜猜是什么！

哦，天啊！好吧，我认为这很明显……

是一只飞机上的鸭子！

不是！

哦。嗯……是农夫吗……还有一只圆滚滚的小猪，也可能是沙滩球？

不——！

啊……一条狗拿着一张彩票？

妈妈！

这部分看起来像监狱围场……是监狱吗……在月光下？

妈咪!

告诉我。
这是一根棍子在吃一颗葡萄!

太棒了，亲爱的。
让我们把它放到壁炉旁
那一大堆东西里。
那是妈妈所有
专题论文的去处。

Interpreting your preschool artwork

I made this for you, Mommy!
Honey. It . . . is . . . a-MAZ-ing.
But you're not looking. You're looking at your phone.

Sorry, honey. I see it now.
Guess what it is!
Oh my! Well I think it's pretty obvious . . .
It's a duck on a plane!

No it isn't!
Oh. Well . . . is it a farmer . . . and a little round pig
    who might also be a beach ball?
Noooo!

Ahhh . . . a dog holding a lottery ticket?
Mom!

This part looks like a prison yard . . . Is it a prison . . .
    in the moonlight?

Mommy!

Tell me.
It's a stick eating a grape!

Good job, sweetie.
Let's put it in the big pile
by the fireplace
where all of Mommy's
special papers go.

周末与家人共进早餐

我在周日早起,
洗了两大堆衣服,
列了下一周的
购物清单,
为每个人
做了鸡蛋和煎饼。

我的孩子们拥抱了我。
多么可爱。

你是软屁股夫人,
我的女儿说,
一边捏着我的屁股,
笑着。

我儿子和丈夫也笑了。

是啊,妈妈!
你的屁股太软了!

整栋房子里你屁股最软！

每个人都在笑
说着我有个
多软的屁股。
多有趣！

只不过我想我有点儿累。
周末有时很漫长，
而我去健身房的次数
也许也不够多。

当我把
装煎饼面糊的碗
扔进水槽，
大喊着
"你们都给我下地狱"时，
你们都不笑了。

我可能反应过度了。

Weekend breakfast with the family

I was up early on Sunday
and did two loads of laundry
and made a shopping list
for the week
and then made eggs and pancakes
for everyone.

My children hugged me.
How lovely.

You're Mrs. Squishy Butt
my daughter said
squeezing my butt
laughing.

My son and husband laughed too.

You are, Mom!
Your butt is so squishy!

You have the squishiest butt in the whole house!

Everyone kept laughing
and saying I had
a squishy butt.
What fun!

Except I guess I was a bit tired.
The weekends can be long.
And maybe I don't go to the gym
as much as I should.

You all stopped laughing though
when I threw the bowl
of pancake batter
into the sink
and shouted
You can all go straight to hell!

I may have overreacted.

我们之间的热度

孩子们睡下之后，
在厨房，
终于只剩我俩了。

你穿着松松垮垮的运动裤、
脏兮兮的羊毛衫
和旧袜子。
我能感受到你的性感，
如果只用余光去看。

"我好兴奋"，
我听到你说，
嘴里含着一大口
直接从锅里舀出来的
凉芝士通心粉。

累。
你说："我好累。"
是我的错。

我俯身亲吻你的脖子，
被一阵浓烈的气味击中，
我退后了几步。
新洗发水？我问。
不，我觉得是孩子吐奶弄的。

我感受到我们之间的热度。
那是灶台上的火，
我忘了关，
我错了。

The heat between us

In the kitchen
after the babies are down
we are finally alone.

You in your baggy sweatpants
stained fleece
and old socks.
I sense your sexuality.
If I squint.

I am so turned on
I hear you say
through a mouthful
of cold mac and cheese
spooned directly from a saucepan.

Tired.
You said *I am so tired.*
My bad.

I lean in to kiss your neck
and am hit with a powerful scent
that forces me back.
New shampoo? I ask.
No. I think that's spit-up.

I feel the heat between us.
And that heat is the front burner
which I left on by mistake.

凌晨三点三十二分，我打赌婴儿在嘲笑我

海豹突击队会做一件事，
我听说，
是魔鬼周训练。
白天和黑夜
几乎没有睡眠，
他们到达了极限。

不过这种训练只持续五天。
这使我发笑，
当我站在浴室里，
穿着内衣，
开着淋浴，
抱着你时。

为什么？
因为你，
小宝宝，
喜欢水的声音。

而你根本不睡觉，
这是你第三次起来了，
完全清醒地
看着我，
就像海豹突击队的教官，
等着我崩溃。

我再次嘲笑特种部队，
多么窝囊。
生个孩子试试！我想。

为什么不带一个婴儿参加战斗呢！
我说最后这句话的时候声音很大，
注意到我的妻子站在门口。

把孩子给我，她平静地说。

我看着我怀里的婴儿
刚在我身上吐了一口，
好像无声地说了句"蠢货"，
对此我十分确定。

3:32 A.M. and I am sure the infant is taunting me

The Navy SEALs do a thing
so I have heard.
Hell Week.
Days and nights
with almost no sleep.
Pushed to their limit.

Except it only lasts five days.
This makes me laugh
as I stand holding you
in the bathroom
in my underwear
with the shower running.

Why?
Because you
tiny baby
like the sound of the water.

But you won't go to sleep.
And this is the third time you've been up
wide-awake
looking at me
like an instructor at SEAL training
waiting for me to crack.

I laugh again at what weenies
the Special Forces are.
Get a baby! I think.

Take an infant baby into combat why don't you!
Except I say that last part out loud.
And notice my wife standing at the door.

Give me the baby, she says quietly.

I look at my little bundle
who spits up on me
and appears to mouth *dickhead.*
I am sure of it.

谢谢你

致
好心的
在我后面
排队的
老女人，
她无微不至地教我，
当我的小孩
崩溃时
我应该做什么。

没有冒犯的意思，
不过说真的：
去你妈的。

Thank you

To the
kindly
older woman
behind me
in line
at CVS
who lectured me
extensively
about what I *should* do
while my toddler was
having a
meltdown.

No offense
but seriously
kiss my ass.

纽约飞洛杉矶

女士们先生们，
现在是机长
在驾驶舱讲话。
今天去往洛杉矶的飞行时间
为六小时十五分钟，
但对于那些带着孩子旅行的人来说，
会感到飞行时间有两倍那么长。

我已经关闭了"系好安全带"的标识，
所以请随便让您的
孩子来回跑，
五十或一百趟，
直到您
与您同机的乘客
及机组人员
精疲力竭。

头顶的行李舱应保持关闭，
除非您意识到需要检查装有尿不湿的背包，

翻来翻去才发现它被托运了。

如果与您坐在一起的人吐在您身上，
请知悉您的衣服
也已装在了托运行李中。

现在只需坐下，
大哭一场，
在飞行中感受痛苦。

JFK–LAX

Ladies and gentlemen
from the flight deck
this is your captain speaking.
Flight time today to Los Angeles
is six hours and fifteen minutes
but will feel twice that long
for those of you traveling with children.

I've turned the *fasten seat belt* sign off
so please feel free to let your
toddlers roam up and back
fifty or one hundred times
exhausting you
your fellow passengers
and the flight crew.

The overhead bins should be kept closed
until you need to rifle through them swearing
only to realize you checked the bag with the diapers.

If you are seated with someone who vomits on you
please know that your clothes
are also in the checked bag.

Now just sit back
burst into tears
and feel miserable during the flight.

做得好

我经常对你说这句话，
在足球比赛的绿茵场边，
在校园剧表演之后，
在你自己倒了一杯水时。

就好像你刚刚研造了化油器。

想知道真相吗？
你在足球比赛中表现得并不好，
你让那个狡猾的小屁孩超过你进了球。
你干吗非要跟他赛跑呢？
也许下次应该把他直接放倒。

你也不是梅丽尔·斯特里普。
老师不得不把台词一句句教给你，
坦率地说，这令人难以置信。

我知道跟你说这些的时候，
是你五岁的生日，
但我想有一天你会感谢我的。

Good job

I say these words so often to you.
From the sidelines of soccer games.
After the school play.
When you get a glass of water by yourself.

As if you just rebuilt a carburetor.

Want to know the truth?
You didn't do a very good job in soccer.
You let that little weaselly kid get by you and score.
Why were you running along beside him, anyway?
Maybe take him down next time.

And Meryl Streep you're not.
The teacher had to feed you the lines
which were, frankly, unconvincing.

I know I'm saying this to you
on your fifth birthday.
But I think you'll thank me one day.

给我青春期孩子们的饮酒建议

你们现在是高中生了，
派对，朋友，
可能要喝酒的场合，
不要觉得有压力。
看看我是怎么做的。
我下班回家
多半要喝杯冰镇啤酒。
没什么大不了的，
一杯啤酒而已，
一仰脖就下肚了。爽。
见鬼，也许我要再来一杯啤酒，
两杯就是所谓的"适量"。
喝完了。
或者我也许会想：
嘿，这是星期二的晚上，放轻松。
杜松子酒配汤力水可以做我朋友。
温暖的天气，很好，
数九寒天也很好，
照样杜松子酒配汤力水。

再加点儿青柠，文明人的配方。

我是在自己家里，没在开车，而且可能也没穿裤子。

也许我热了一个卷饼，然后去地下室看比赛，

因为你妈妈说过

"到地下室去看比赛"。

你知道卷饼配什么最好吗？

葡萄酒，一杯葡萄酒。

一小杯就好。

《圣经》里也提到葡萄酒了，你知道吗？

喝一点儿对你没任何坏处。

可以再来一杯。

投入地看着比赛。工作一天很辛苦，好好享受。

现在可能已经很晚了。

你看到我地下室的那瓶白兰地了吗？

来那么一点儿，

就当睡前饮品。

也许睡在地窖里的躺椅上，用沙滩巾当毯子盖上。

我的意思是，你们要小心点儿对待酒这种东西。

Advice to my teenage children on drinking

You're in high school now.

Parties. Friends.

Events where there might be alcohol.

Don't feel pressure to drink.

Look at me.

I come home from work

and I might have a cold beer.

No big deal.

One beer.

Goes down easy. Cold.

Heck, maybe I have a second beer.

Two beers is what's called moderation.

Done.

Or maybe I think

Hey. It's Tuesday night. Let your hair down.

A gin and tonic can be a friend.

Warm weather. Nice.

Or even the dead of winter.

One gin and tonic.

Throw in a lime. Civilized.

I'm home. I'm not driving. And at this point I'm
probably not wearing pants.

Maybe I heat up a burrito and go into the basement
to watch a game

because your mother has said

Go to the basement and watch a game.

You know what's nice with a burrito?

Wine. Maybe a glass of wine.

Small glass.

Wine is in the Bible. Did you know that?

Little bit won't kill you.

Maybe a second glass of wine.

Into the game. Hard day at work. Relaxing.

It's probably late now.

Have you seen that bottle of cognac I have in the
basement?

Tiny drop of that.

Nightcap.

Maybe sleep in the cellar on the lounge chair with a
beach towel as a blanket.

My point is you want to be careful with this stuff.

我们约个时间做爱吧

周二晚上你可以吗?

可以的。糟糕,不行。我预约了健身课,还要去"橙色理论"。

嗯,好吧。周三晚上?等等,不行。周三我要陪客户吃晚饭。

周四我在波士顿。

我周五早上回家上班前还有时间。

好的。见鬼,不行。我要去乔氏超市,然后带孩子们去看牙。

周六……

别想。足球,棒球,还有两个生日派对。

星期天早上?让他们看电视去?

认真的吗?你不想好好睡一觉吗?

说得好。

上班时打电话调情?

办公室里到处都是人,不可以。

那现在呢?

我不懂。

我们可以现在做爱,难道不是吗?

现在……你是说……现在?

那很疯狂吗?

是有点儿疯狂。我的意思是……亲爱的……这不在日
程表上啊。

你说得完全没错。算了吧。

Let's schedule a time for sex

Would Tuesday evening work for you?

Yes. Shoot. No. I have a P.T.A. meeting and then Orangetheory.

Hmm. Okay. Wednesday night? Wait. Nope. Wednesday I have a client dinner.

Thursday I'm in Boston.

I could do Friday morning after drop-off and before work.

Yes. Shit. No. I'm going to Trader Joe's then the kids' dentist.

Saturday . . .

Don't be insane. Soccer, baseball, and two birthday parties.

Sunday morning? Put them in front of screens?

Really? Wouldn't you rather sleep in?

Good point.

Phone sex from the office?

Open work space. Can't.

What about now?

I don't understand.

We could have sex now. Couldn't we?

Now . . . like . . . now?

Is that crazy?

It's a little crazy. I mean . . . honey . . . it's not on the
    calendar.

You're totally right. Forget it.

你以为打完七小时
高尔夫去小憩一下是个好主意

你周六一早就走了，
把孩子们丢给我。
整整一天。
男孩子们一直在吵架，
小儿子抱着我的腿哭个不停。

你回家正好赶上孩子午睡，
而我带双胞胎去游泳了，
所以你以为一切都好。
我们回来后，你的宿醉开始发作了。

"我想吃点儿巧克力味的脆脆的东西。"
你对我说，
在厨房，
挠着你的屁股。

"我不知道，威化饼干之类的？
家里有这种东西吗？

或者我就吃巧克力蛋糕。"

我想我的表情和沉默
都告诉了你家里没有，
你也不该吃。

所以你宣布是时候"稍稍躺下休息一会儿"了。

喝了一天酒的成年男人都会睡午觉吗？
很显然，他们会。
哦，但你猜怎么着？
成年女人可以让孩子们去
扑向爸爸
并且把你该死地吵醒。

**You thought it would be a good idea to take a
nap after a seven-hour golf outing**

You leave early Saturday morning.
And I have the kids.
All day.
The boys fight.
Our youngest remains glued to my legs the whole time
    crying.

You get home just in time for the baby's nap.
So you get to cover that
while I take the twins to swimming.
We get back and now your hangover is starting to kick in.

I feel like something chocolaty and crispy
you say to me
in the kitchen
scratching your ass.

I dunno, like a wafer of some kind?

Do we have anything like that?
Or I'll take chocolate cake.

I guess my expression and silence
tell you we don't
and you won't.

So you announce that it's time for a *little lie-down*.

Do adult men who day-drink get to take naps?
Apparently, they do.
Oh but guess what?
Adult women get to tell the kids to
jump on Daddy and
wake you the hell up.

星期六晚上

我听说
有的人
在晚上
出门。
工作日晚上。
周末晚上。

他们去
餐馆。
他们去看演出。
有时既去餐馆也去看演出，
在同一个晚上。
不，我不知道他们是怎么做到这一点的。

他们没有在晚上七点随便穿件睡衣，
看半部他们可能已经看过的电影，
到了九点才开始使劲打哈欠。

我们以前经常出去玩吗？

我是说从家里出去?

还是我记错人了?

我们是从什么时候开始九点半就睡觉的?

也许我们可以明早谈谈这个问题,

眼下

我是相当困了。

Saturday night

I have heard
that there are people
who go out
at night.
Weeknights.
Weekends.

They go to
restaurants.
They go to shows.
Sometimes both
in the same evening.
And no, I do not know how they do this.

They do not change
into some form of pajama-wear by 7 P. M.
and watch half of a movie they've likely already seen
only to begin convulsively yawning by 9.

Did we used to go out?

Of the house, I mean?

Or am I thinking of someone else?

When did we start going to bed at 9:30?

Perhaps we can talk about this

in the morning

as right now

I am quite sleepy.

离家一英里之后，
你问我们的防晒霜装好了没有

真的吗？

这就是你的问题？

我们记得带防晒霜了吗？

是的，我们带了。

该怎么表达我的感受呢？

当我装好

防晒霜、

防虫喷雾器

和三明治，

还有你的两罐啤酒时，

你窝在沙发上，

穿着内衣，

盯着你的手机看。

我看了看你，

琢磨该如何回应。

但是你又问了
一个在我看来
很好的问题。

"孩子们在哪儿?"

A mile from the house, you ask if we've packed the sunscreen

Really?
That's your question?
Did *we* remember to pack the sunscreen?

Yup, *we* did.

How to express how that makes me feel
since while I packed
the sunscreen
and the bug spray
and the sandwiches
and your two cans of beer
you sat on the couch
in your underwear
and stared at your phone.

I look at you
searching for the right response.

But then you ask
what I think
is a pretty great question.

Where are the children?

早起的鸟儿

一个冬日的早晨，
又黑又冷。

你走进卧室
宣告：

"我睡得特别差劲。
我的鼻子被塞住了，
我他妈的简直没法呼吸。"

的确
我是英国人，
而且也许
偶尔
我骂人。

但是你
才两岁半啊。

虽然我们为你的口才

感到自豪，

但是我们也有点儿担心。

Early riser

A winter morning
cold and dark.

You come into the bedroom
with an announcement.

I had such a bad sleep.
My nose is stuffed up
and I can't fucking breathe.

Now granted
I am English
and perhaps
I curse
on occasion.

But you are
only two and a half.

And while we are proud
of your verbal skills
we're also a bit concerned.

表示爱慕的词语

蜜糖。甜心。亲爱的。
南瓜。松饼。小绵羊。

这些词语我从没用在你身上，
从来没有。
相反，我有我自己的一套昵称。

"你"。
我有时会这么叫你。

"嘿你"，这是个好名字。
或者"对，就是他"。

"我丈夫"。很亲密，对不对？

或者"加里"——我是说"莱纳德"。
两个名字里都有 a，我有时会搞不清楚。

"哦，艾伦！"我曾经这么叫过你，你一直都没让我忘记。那是个错误，我已经道过歉了。

Terms of endearment

Honey. Sweetheart. Darling.
Pumpkin. Muffin. Lamb chop.

These are names I never use for you.
Ever.
Instead, I have my own pet names.

You.
I call you that sometimes.

You over there. That's a good one.
Or *Yup, that's him.*

My husband. That's intimate, isn't it?

Or *Gary.* I mean *Leonard.*
Both have the letter "a" in them and I get confused
    sometimes.

Oh, Alan! I called you that once and you've never let
　　me forget it.

That was a mistake and I apologized for that.

你说什么

你能在同志食府腌鱼吃吗?
你问。
至少我觉得你是这么问的。
我们卧室里的空调又破又吵,
而你背对着我,
我们俩还都没有完全清醒。

什么? 我问。
你能在五点十五接孩子吗?
哦,好的,我说。

那条鲤鱼正和特德在地下打仗。
那是什么?
那辆汽车又开始嘎吱嘎吱地响。
我会去找修车师傅。

伊朗怪罪萨尔曼·鲁西迪。
等一下,什么?
我想我晚餐要吃三文鱼。

听起来不错。

哦，还有我怀孕了。
现在我听明白了。
你是说这里的天气太阴？
不，我说我怀孕了。
你错过了那部电影？
亲爱的，我，怀，孕，了。

真奇怪，我怎么就是听不明白。

What did you say?

Can you pickle the kippers near the gay canteen?
you ask.
At least I think that's what you ask.
The air conditioner in our bedroom is old and noisy
and your back is to me.
Neither of us fully awake.

What? I say.
Can you pick up the kids at 5:15?
Oh. Okay, I say.

And the carp is battling the underground with Ted.
What's that?
The car is making that rattling sound again.
I'll bring it to the mechanic.

Iran takes Salman Rushdie for a sinner.
Wait. What?
I was thinking I'd make that salmon for dinner.

Sounds good.

Oh. And I'm pregnant.

I get it now.

You mean the air in here is stagnant?

No. I said I'm pregnant.

You miss the show *Dragnet*?

Honey. I. Am. Pregnant.

Weird. I'm just not getting it.

致马可，一个帅哥同事，他常调情，并说些"妈妈们都很性感"之类的话，诚然这听起来很怪异，但你不得不听他说，因为他是巴西人

阿——莉——森，他说，细细品味着我名字中的每一个发音。

他走到我办公桌旁站在我身后，让我很惊讶。

他身上有一股海雾或松树的味道，或者是用了爽身粉。

不管是什么味道，他都洒了很多。

哦，嘿，马可，我说得太随意了。

马可慢慢地点点头，用他独有的方式盯着我看。

无害的打情骂俏。

我已经告诉了我老公，菲尔，马可是我的办公室迷恋对象。

阿——莉——森，他又说。

我让菲尔用巴西口音念过我的名字，

但他来自费城，太可怕了。
艾尔，菲尔这么叫。
艾尔是个男人的名字，我不是男人。

马可用一种菲尔没用过的方式看着我。
我们是灵魂伴侣吗？

然后马可说：
从你那圆滚滚的大肚子，我看得出你又怀孕了。

不，我说，那只是我的肚子。
我恨马可。

哦，马可说，是的……好吧……你的考勤表已经过期了。
马可彻底玩完了。

**To Marco, the hot guy at work who flirts
and says things like *Moms are sexy*, which
admittedly sounds creepy, but you have to hear
him say it because he's Brazilian**

A-lee-son, he says, savoring every sound in my name.
He has come up behind me at my desk, surprising me.

He smells of sea spray or pine trees or maybe toner.
Whatever it is he's used a lot of it.

Oh hey, Marco, I say too casually.
Marco is nodding slowly, staring at me in that way he has.

Harmless flirting.
I've told my husband, Phil, that Marco is my office crush.

A-lee-son, he says again.
I asked Phil to say my name with a Brazilian accent
but he's from Philly and it was horrible.
Al, Phil says.

Al is a man's name. I am not a man.

Marco sees me in a way Phil does not.
Are we soul mates?

Then Marco says
I see from your big round belly that you are pregnant again.

No, I say. *That's just my belly.*
I hate Marco.

Oh, Marco says. *Yes . . . well . . . your time sheets are past
    due.*
Marco is dead to me.

你自己的歌

你赞美你自己，歌唱你自己
你承担的也想让我承担[1]。
这话谁说的？
或是类似的什么话？
沃尔特·惠特曼？
可是，老沃尔特不会在你旁边喋喋不休，
在你下班的路上
给你讲述他的一天。
会议，
电话会议，
参加电话会议的人，
你在普里特吃的火腿三明治。
告诉我更多事吧！
在我做晚饭，你吃饼干的时候。
不，我想我们没有蘸酱。
我们以前有蘸酱吗？
孩子们已经洗完澡，吃好饭，准备睡觉了。
你记得我们有孩子，对吧？
而我就在这里。

我也过了一整天。

这是真的。

你可以问问我今天过得怎么样。

不?

我的错。

请一定要告诉我你老板关于"裤子"的段子。

---

1 此句原文为："我赞美我自己，歌唱我自己，我承担的你也将承担。"出自沃尔特·惠特曼的诗《自己的歌》。——编者注

Song of yourself

You celebrate yourself and sing yourself
and what you assume you want me to assume.
Who said that?
Or something like that?
Walt Whitman?
Well, old Walt wouldn't get in a word edgewise with you
walking in from work
and telling him about your day.
The meetings
the conference calls
who was on the conference calls
the ham sandwich you had from Pret.
Tell me more!
As I make dinner and you eat crackers.
No, I don't think we have any dip.
Have we ever had dip?
The kids are bathed and fed and ready for bed.
You remember we have kids, right?
And I'm here.

And I had a day too.

It's true.

You could ask me how my day was.

No?

My bad.

Definitely tell me the funny thing your boss said
    about the word "pants."

我不知道我们为什么要去露营

那似乎是个好主意。
那天晚上我们做好了计划,
但如果没记错的话,
我们当时在屋里,
喝着酒,
上着网,
看网上介绍了非常棒的露营地。

我们一定要去露营!
我们是这么喜欢露营的人!

只是现在,
我们在野外,
在黑暗中,
天还下着雨。
现在还没到晚上九点,
也没有什么事可做。
我们躺在地上。
大自然的夜晚总是这么吵闹吗?

我又热又冷。

一切都脏兮兮的。

大家都离得太近了。

我们女儿的口气闻起来像流浪汉的脚。

有东西在我脸上爬来爬去。

原来

我们不是

喜欢露营的人。

知道这一点真是太好了。

I don't know why we went camping

It seemed like a good idea
that night we planned it.
But if memory serves
we were indoors
drinking
looking at a website
of amazing campsites.

We should definitely go camping!
We're such camping people!

Except now
we are outdoors
in the dark
and the rain.
It's not yet 9 P. M.
and there is nothing to do.
And we are lying on the ground.
Has nature always been this loud at night?

I am both hot and cold.

And so unclean.

Everyone is too close.

Our daughter's breath smells like a homeless man's feet.

Something is crawling on my face.

It turns out

we are not

camping people.

Good to know.

有关我最近社交网站上
大峡谷照片的一些背景资料

谢谢你的

点赞和评论。

完美的家庭！

太幸福了！

多么漂亮的小男孩和小女孩！

这些照片很精彩，

但照片是很有趣的东西，

因为它们会说谎。

举个例子。

我们两个孩子骑马的那张？

他们刚刚在

进行一场尖叫比赛，

因为玛丽·帕特

用马鞭抽打她哥哥贾瑞德，

导致他落马。

马受惊脱缰，

而我们可爱的老导游说，

去他的 。

还有那张我和格伦微笑的照片？

假的。

事实上，

在拍这张照片不到五秒钟前，

我告诉他，

他是个傻鸟。

你知道我为什么这么说吗？

因为他就是。

虽然我不相信

拍这张照片的那群修女

知道什么是"傻鸟"。

那些沙漠美景的照片

都是在开车返回

烂旅馆，

没有人说话的时候拍的。

然而我们确实看起来很完美。

让你有这样的感觉，

这当然是我们的本意。

Some background on those recent Grand Canyon photos I posted on Instagram

Thank you
for the likes and comments.
Perfect family!
So happy!
Such handsome teenage kids!

They were wonderful photos.
But pictures are funny things.
Because they lie.

For example.
The one of our two teenagers on horseback?
They'd just been in
a screaming match
because Mary-Pat had
whipped her older brother Jared with a riding crop
causing him to fall off his horse
the horse bolting

and our lovely elderly guide saying
Screw this.

And that picture of Glen and me smiling?
Faked.
In fact, I had just told him
not five seconds before the photo
that he was a *dickhead.*
Do you know why I told him that?
Because he is.
Though I don't believe that
the group of nuns who took the photo
knew the word "dickhead."

The scenic desert shots
are from the drive back to the
crappy motel
when no one spoke.

We did look perfect though.
And that was certainly our intention
to make you feel that way.

我试着在家里采取家庭治疗师的建议

确认。
主动忽略。
痛苦忍受。

我不知道这些词是什么意思，
但在治疗师的办公室里我点了点头，
我的妻子一边做笔记一边问着问题。

治疗室里有香氛蜡烛
和佛教经旗，
还有一个小喷泉。

我们家没有这些东西。
我家有两个十几岁的孩子，
还有一个脏兮兮的厨房，
以及没完成的家庭作业。

"虽然你容易情绪失控，菲尔，但你可以冷静下来！"
治疗师说。

那好吧。

我们来试试。

嘿，儿子，

你真擅长把平板电脑关掉。

我为你真实的样子感到骄傲。

我是说，你是一个人。

是时候把它关掉了，而这件事你很擅长，

就像你擅长生活中的很多其他事情一样。

请关掉它吧，好孩子。

做得好，差点儿就把它关掉了！

你到底有没有听到我说的？

就……点点头……或者有点儿别的表示。

看，在你积极主动地无视我的时候，

我也在积极主动地无视你。

这不是很好吗？

嘿，老兄？

格雷格？

格雷格。

格雷格，把该死的平板电脑关了，不然我就把它扔到该

死的窗户外面去。

好了。

现在回你的房间去吧。

务请从速。

做得好。

I attempt to employ the family therapist's suggestions at home

Validation.

Active ignoring.

Distress tolerance.

I don't know what these words mean.

But I nodded in the therapist's office

as my wife took notes and asked questions.

The office had scented candles

and Buddhist prayer flags

and a small fountain.

We don't have any of those things in our house.

We have two teenagers.

And a dirty kitchen.

And unfinished homework.

Despite your emotionally stunted self, Phil, you can be calm!

the therapist had said.

Okay then.

Let's try.

Hey, son.

You are so good at turning that iPad off.

I'm so proud of who you are.

As a person, I mean.

Time to turn it off now, which you are so good at

like so many other things in your life.

Off please, good son.

Good job almost turning it off!

Are you hearing me at all?

Just . . . nod . . . or something please.

Look at me actively ignoring you

while you actively ignore me.

Isn't this good? Hey, bud?

Greg?

Greg.

Greg, turn the fucking iPad off or I'll throw it out

the Goddamned window.

There we go.

Now go to your room.

At your earliest convenience.

Good job.

你觉得你真会搬出家门吗

嘿，爸爸，我们又没酸奶了，
你说，
用这种打招呼的方式，
在我下班回家的时候。

而我所说的"班"
指的是职业。
我说的"职业"
指的是能养家糊口的东西。
算了，这不重要。

还有其他东西要买吗，我大学毕业的二十六岁孩子？
多力多滋农场玉米片和真菌软膏。
知道了。
哦，还有小熊软糖。
记下了。

还有些事要提醒你。
我在你这个年纪已经结婚并有了两个孩子。

还记得你爷爷吗?

他十八岁的时候参加了"二战"。

我确信他们没有在他家里打仗,

这意味着他不得不离开家,

去了欧洲。

战争是在那里进行的。

你想去打仗吗?

也许尝试一下?

谁他妈的喝了我剩下的无糖饮料粉? 你问。

我不知道,儿子。

我什么都不知道。

我和你妈妈会在后院里

抬头看天空,

弄明白我们哪里做错了。

Is your sense that you will ever move out of the house?

Hey, Dad, we're out of yogurt again
you say
by way of a greeting
when I get home from work.

And by "work"
I mean a job.
And by "job"
I mean something you get to earn money.
Never mind.

Anything else, my college-educated
      twenty-six-year-old?
Cool Ranch Doritos and fungal cream.
Got it.
Oh and gummy bears.
Noted.

And here's something for you to note.
I was married with two kids when I was your age.

And remember your granddad?
He was in World War II when he was eighteen.
And I'm pretty sure they didn't fight the war in his
        house.
Which means he had to move out to Europe.
Where the war was.

Would you want to go to war?
Maybe try that?

Who drank the rest of my freakin' Crystal Light? you ask.

I don't know, son.
I don't know anything anymore.
Your mother and I will be in the backyard
staring into space
wondering where we went wrong.

星期天开车

长途驾车可以是一种度过整个下午的有趣方式。
佛罗里达的那个女人无疑这么认为。
她开车，开车，开车。
多么有趣！

很显然，她和她丈夫刚刚吵了一架。
她离开了家，
而他跳上了她的汽车引擎盖。
那是个错误。

他坚持认为她会停下来。
她的丈夫紧紧抓着引擎盖，她能开多远？

答案是很远，
一直开到了州际公路上，
以高达每小时七十英里的速度行驶。

大约二十英里后，警察终于把她拦住了。

那个男人没事。

他们说，经过心理咨询和一段时间的修整，他可以恢复正常的生活。

这不是很好笑吗？

你为什么不笑？

你为什么这样看着我？

要不要去开车兜兜风？

Sunday drive

A long drive can be a lovely way to spend an
    afternoon.
That woman in Florida certainly thought so.
She drove and drove and drove.
What fun!

Apparently, she and her husband had just had a
    fight.
She left the house
and he jumped on the hood of her car.
That was a mistake.

He clung on thinking that she would stop.
How far could she drive with her husband hanging
    on to the hood?

A long way is the answer.
All the way to the interstate.
At speeds of up to seventy miles per hour.

After about twenty miles the police finally stopped
   her.
The man was fine.
They say with counseling and time he could resume
   a normal life.

Isn't it hilarious?
Why aren't you laughing?
Why are you looking at me like that?
Want to go for a drive?

在波士顿长大并不是你那样做的借口 [1]

我知道你是在哪里长大的。
我见过你的家人
和朋友，
我很清楚他们不正常的事实。

但你是个成年男人，
成了家，
而我们也不住在波士顿。

所以你不能在看冰球比赛时
对着电视大喊大叫：
去他妈的游骑兵队！
我不知道那是什么意思。
人们不会说这样的话，
即使孩子不在场时也是如此。

难道你真的希望
纽约洋基队里的

每个人
都食物中毒？
你为什么要这么说？

是的，汤姆·布雷迪[2]很有才华，
但我不认为
他是个多重要的历史人物，
跟甘地相比。

再提醒我一下，
什么是"寸货"[3]？

---

1 这首诗拿美国人对"波士顿人"的固化印象开了玩笑。很多波士顿
  人爱好体育，爱说一些土话，自带口音，因此常常会被调侃。——
  编者注
2 汤姆·布雷迪：美国橄榄球运动员，波士顿人。——编者注
3 原文为"ahhs-hole"，调侃了波士顿口音，意为"蠢货"。

Saying you grew up in Boston is not an excuse for your behavior

I know where you grew up.
I have met your family
and friends
and I am well aware of the fact that they are not
  normal.

But you are a grown man
with a family
and we don't live in Boston.

So you cannot scream at the television
during a hockey game and say
Fuck the Rangers!
I don't know what that means.
That's not a thing people say
even when children aren't in the room.

And do you really hope

that every member of
the New York Yankees
gets food poisoning?
Why would you say that?

Yes, Tom Brady is talented.
But I disagree that
he is a more important historical figure
than Gandhi.

Remind me again.
What's an *ahhs-hole*, anyway?

那东西在哪里

那东西在哪里？

你问我，

往炉子上方的柜子里看着。

新的还是旧的？我问，

相当确定你明白我的意思。

旧的那个。

在水槽下面。

它不在那里。

看一下就找到了。

我看着呢。

看那玩意儿下面。

它不在这里。

另一个玩意儿。

没有。

等等，你是说绿色的那个？

不，是蓝色的。我认为是蓝色的。

哦，那个在抽屉里。

我检查过抽屉了。

你检查过那个塑料的东西后面了吗？

我们说的是同一件东西，对吧，顶部很怪异的那个？

当然了。

等等，它在这里。

Where's that thing?

Where's that thing?
you ask me
looking in the cabinet above the stove.
The new one or *old one*, I reply,
fairly sure you know what I mean.
Old one.
Under the sink.
It's not there.
Just look.
I'm looking.
Look under that stuff.
It's not here.
The other stuff.
Nope.
Wait. You mean the green one?
No. Blue. I think it's blue.
Oh. That's in the drawer.
I checked the drawer.
Did you check behind the plastic thing?

We're talking about the same thing, right, the one with the
weird top?

Of course.

Wait. Here it is.

《无用的人》前情提要

有时候，我觉得我可以写一部电视剧。
我有想法，
我一直在构思。

看看下面这个。

试播剧集会发生在一个家庭中，
故事发生在孩子们准备上学的时候。
我们看到那个女人在做午餐，
帮孩子们在上课前完成家庭作业、
系鞋带、
背上背包、
舀麦片。
我们看到那个男人拿着他的平板电脑坐在马桶上。

当母亲和孩子们离开家去学校的时候，
这名男子尝试着从马桶上站起来，
但他已经坐了这么久，

他的腿麻木了。

然后他在那里待了一天。

片尾字幕滚动。

Previously on *Useless Man*

Sometimes I think I could write a TV show.
I have ideas
that come to me all the time.

Here's one.

The pilot episode would take place in a home
as the children were getting ready for school.
We see the woman making lunches
helping with last-minute homework
tying shoes
packing backpacks
spooning cereal.
We see the man on the toilet on his iPad.

As the mother and children leave for school
the man tries to stand from the toilet.
But he's been sitting for so long

his legs have gone numb.

And he's stuck there all day.

Credits roll.

请不要拿我和我妈妈比

当你说我表现得像我妈妈一样时，

你是想让我发疯吗？

你一定是。

你知道我妈妈其实是个疯子。

她曾经在银行抢劫案中开过那辆逃逸车，

我姐姐就坐在后面的儿童座椅上。

（她没有被起诉。）

还有一次她把我们家的房子刷成黑色来惹我爸爸生气。

她还在院子里用弓弩射杀松鼠，因为她觉得它们在

"听"她说话。

她还担心联合国前秘书长布特罗斯·布特罗斯－加利在

跟踪她。

所以当我因为汽车电池又没电了而大发雷霆的时候，

请不要拿我和我妈妈相比。

她目前因重大盗窃罪被判处五年徒刑。

而且我是个男人。

Please don't compare me to my mother

When you say that I am acting just like my mother
do you want me to go insane?
You must.
You know my mother is actually insane.
And that she drove the getaway car in a bank robbery
    once
with my older sister in the toddler seat in back
(she was not charged).
And once painted our house black to annoy my father.
And used a crossbow on squirrels in the yard because
    she felt they were "listening" to her.
And worried that former U.N. Secretary General
    Boutros Boutros-Ghali was following her.
So when I get angry that the car battery has died again
    and throw a hissy fit
please don't compare me to my mother.
Who is currently serving a five-year sentence for grand
    larceny.
Also I am a man.

致我的第五个孩子

我当然知道你的名字，
只是有时，
它会帮助我
先把其他孩子的名字都说完，
在我说你的名字之前。
我知道和哥哥姐姐们相比，
你小时候的照片
没有那么多。
而你的
圣诞袜是唯一一只非手工缝制的，
而你的名字
（我知道你的名字！）
写在了被涂掉的"男宝宝"一词上面。
还有，是的，
我们把你丢在了机场，
那次在法国的时候，
但这并不意味着，
我们对你的爱更少，
先生。

这只是意味着我们对你的爱没那么多。
这句话说错了。
而且是的，我说了"先生"，
因为我刚才想不起你的名字。

To my fifth child

Of course I know your name.
It just helps me,
sometimes,
to say all of the others first
before I get to yours.
I know there aren't as many photos
of you as a baby
as there are of your older brothers and sisters.
And that yours is the only
Christmas stocking not handmade
and instead has your name
(which I know!)
written over the words "boy child."
And yes
we left you in the airport
in France that one time.
But that does *not* mean
we love you any less,
mister.

It just means we don't love you quite as much.

That came out wrong.

And yes, I said "mister"

because I couldn't think of your name right then.

挽歌

我们聚集在这里，
在楼上浴室里，
怀念我们的宠物达里尔
相当平淡无奇的一生。
你带给我们一种类似喜悦的感觉，
在我们认识你的这十一天里——
如果"喜悦"是指
我们的孩子
艾丽斯和鲁比求我们把你买下来后，
几乎在
我们从宠物店回家的那一刻开始，
就几乎完全
对你的存在
缺乏兴趣。
而且，
请原谅，
他们一再抱怨说你不是
沙鼠或狗或长颈鹿。

所以，

通过冲水，

我们经过这个马桶把你托付给大海，

附上鲁比送的一把

金鱼饼干。

好了。

不，我们不会养狗。

是的，你们现在可以看《海绵宝宝》了。

Elegy

We are gathered here
in the upstairs bathroom
to honor the remarkably uninteresting life
of our pet Daryl.
You brought us a feeling akin to joy
during the eleven days we knew you.
If by "joy" you mean
an almost complete
lack of interest
in your existence
by our children
Iris and Ruby
from almost the moment
we arrived home from the pet store
after they begged me for you.
Also,
please forgive the many times
they whined that you weren't
a gerbil or a dog or giraffe.

And so

with this flush

we entrust you to the sea

via this toilet

in the company of a handful

of Goldfish crackers

compliments of Ruby.

Okay then.

No we are not getting a dog.

Yes you guys can watch *SpongeBob* now.

尝试总结一个五岁孩子
长篇大论的自言自语

那么让我看看我理解得对不对:
牙仙是不存在的,
因为她没地方放钱。
而且也没有人见过哪个牙仙背着背包,
背包怎么能放上翅膀呢?
有翅膀就不行,你已经试过了。
也许她背的只是个能伸展扩张成大袋子的小袋子,
但她还要装那么多孩子的牙齿呢。
那会有多重?她会崩溃,也许会死。
说得好。

复活节兔子也不可能是真的,
因为它没法拿着篮子,
没有人见过兔子的手,
因为它们没有手。
再说,它们上哪儿去弄鸡蛋和巧克力呢?
那块巧克力是从东京来的,而兔子是不允许上飞机的。
你班上的阿斯特丽德是这么说的。

172

但圣诞老人是真实存在的，有几个原因。
首先，你见过他的照片。
他能飞，这是另一个原因。
他可能原本很瘦，后来才有了个大肚子，
但仍然能钻进任何尺寸的烟囱，
只要没烧火就好。
而谁都不会生火的，
因为那样就拿不到礼物了。

非常有道理。

An attempt at a summation of a five-year-old's monologue

So let me see if I understand.
The tooth fairy makes no sense
because where would she keep the money?
And no one has ever seen a tooth fairy with a
    backpack
because how would a bag fit over her wings?
You can't with wings and you've tried.
Though it could be a tiny pouch that expanded to a
    giant pouch
but still she would have to fit so many kids' teeth
that it would be so heavy she would crash and maybe
    die.
Fair point.

And the Easter bunny can't be real
because how could he hold a basket
because no one has ever seen a rabbit's hands
because they don't have them.

Also, where would they get eggs and chocolate
    anyway
as chocolate is from Tokyo and rabbits aren't even
    allowed on planes.
Astrid in your class says so.

But Santa is real for several reasons.
First, you have seen his picture.
He can fly which is another thing.
And he can be thin and then later have a huge belly
and yet still fit in any standard chimney
as long as it's not on fire
which no one would do because who would want that
when you can get presents instead.

Makes perfect sense.

给夏令营孩子的回信

嗨，甜心，

我很抱歉你讨厌夏令营，

还有你的辅导员、

食物、

你的木屋室友，

和所有的活动。

"酷刑营"会是一个更好的名字，

但你只剩七个星期的时间了，

而且也许雨会在某个时候停下。

你不会错过家中任何好玩的事情，

除非你心血来潮，

觉得去巴黎待五天很有趣。

那的确很有趣。

我们几乎每天晚上都出去吃饭。

我们正在尝试一些新鲜事物，我和你爸爸

早上在后甲板上光着身子喝咖啡，

仅仅是因为我们可以这样做。

哦，我们还把你的卧室粉刷了一遍，

把那些旧的绘画作品都摘掉了，

反正它们也不是很好。(哈哈!)

我们把它变成了一间办公室。

这不是你不能回家的原因。

我们想让你沉浸在大自然中

体验没有屏幕的生活。

说不定九月份的时候你还能去寄宿学校,

那就像为期四年的夏令营。

不是很有趣吗?

坚持住,亲爱的,

我们会在西班牙写信给你的。

Letter back to a summer camper

Hi, sweetheart.

I am so sorry that you hate camp.

As well as your counselor,

the food,

your cabin mates,

and all the activities.

Camp Torture would be a better name.

But you only have seven more weeks.

And maybe it will stop raining at some point.

You're not missing anything fun at home.

Unless you think going to Paris

on a whim for five days is fun.

Which it was.

Also we go out to dinner almost every night.

And we're trying a new thing where your father and I

have coffee naked in the morning on the back deck.

Just because we can.

Oh. And we painted your bedroom.

And took down all that old artwork.

Which was not very good anyway (ha ha!).

And made it into an office.

That's not why you can't come home.

We want you to immerse yourself in nature

and experience life without screens.

And maybe go to boarding school come September.

It would be like summer camp for four years.

Won't that be fun?

Hang in there, sweetie.

We'll write from Spain.

为什么

说实话，

你问的所有问题我几乎都不知道答案。

为什么土豆沙拉里没有生菜？

为什么"马桶"这个词会让你的朋友迈尔斯发笑？

为什么这个世界在这里？

我什么都不知道。

我从事广告业。

如果我整天问你"为什么"呢？

为什么你今天午餐时要坐在凯琳旁边？

为什么诺亚要画一只穿鞋的虫子？

为什么你要假装我们的狗是一个能读心的名叫德米特里
的男人？

为什么吃晚饭时你要把豌豆放在鼻子里？

亲身体验一下我的处境就没那么好玩了吧[1]？

等等。

好玩？

为什么？

---

1 这是一句双关语，也可理解为："鞋子穿反了就没那么好玩了
吧？"——编者注

Why?

I honestly don't know
the answer to almost anything you ask.
Why potato salad doesn't have lettuce in it.
Why the word "toilet" makes your friend Miles
    laugh.
Why the world is here.
I don't know anything.
I work in advertising.
What if I asked you "why" all day?
Why did you sit next to Kalyn at lunch today?
Why did Noah draw a bug with shoes on?
Why did you pretend our dog was a man called
    Dmitri who could read minds?
Why did you put peas in your nose at dinner?
Not so fun when the shoe's on the other foot is it?
Wait.
It is fun?
Why?

致露露

和休伊特

无意冒犯你们两个，
但比起活生生的孩子，
我更喜欢"孩子"这个概念。

当你有九个侄女和侄子的时候，
谁还需要自己的孩子？
你当一阵子的叔叔，
然后就可以一个人回家睡觉了。

都怪你妈妈，
还有她那张漂亮的脸、
那美好的心灵，
还有问及
为什么想要孩子时，
她那完美的回答。

因为我不想再为自己操心了。

我想为别人操心。

我可以告诉你们俩一个秘密吗?

我很害怕。

我怕自己不够好,

太喜怒无常,太没自信,太没耐心,太自私,太乏味。

但后来你们出生了。

你们告诉了我一个秘密。

爸爸,你们轻声说,

你所要做的就是

看着我,倾听我,

牵着我的手,

我就会教你如何做一个父亲。

然后你们就吐在了我的衬衫上。

每天晚上
你们去睡觉前，
我俯下身来，
低声说着同一句话。

在充满疑问
和困惑的一生中，
这是我所知道的最确凿的话。

我很庆幸能做你们的爸爸。

186

For Lulu & Hewitt

No offense to either of you
but I preferred the *idea*
of kids
to actual kids.

Who needs kids of their own
when you have nine nieces and nephews?
You get to be an uncle for a while.
Then you get to go home alone and sleep.

I blame your mother.
And her beautiful face.
And deeply kind spirit.
And her perfect answer
to why she wanted children.

Because I'm tired of worrying about myself.
I want to worry about someone else.

Can I tell you two a secret?
I was afraid.
I was afraid I wouldn't be good enough.
Too moody too needy too impatient too selfish too
    lacking.

But then you were born.
And you told me a secret.

Dad, you whispered.
All you have to do is
watch me and listen to me
and take my hand.
And I'll teach you how to be a father.

Then you spit up on my shirt.

Every night
before you go to sleep
I lean down and
whisper the same sentence.

In a lifetime of questions
and confusion
they are the truest words I know.

I am so lucky to be your dad.

致谢

我要感谢凯茜 s.，她是我上一本书《今晚……要么早点睡》亚马逊网站上的评论者，她说："这本书是最糟糕的。"同时也要感谢罗素公共图书馆的好心人，不管这座图书馆究竟在哪里，他们 **"非常讨厌这本书"**（是他们加粗的，不是我）。他们还说："这本书是垃圾。"谢谢你们，凯茜和罗素公共图书馆的所有人，谢谢你们的不信任。这几乎就像回到了小时候。

感谢普特南出版社的总裁伊万·霍尔德，在《今晚……要么早点睡》成为《纽约时报》畅销书的那一刻起，他终于看好了前者，并立即为这本书开了绿灯。由于第一本书的成功，伊万现在住在法国南部，他在那里画有三个乳房的女人。（可能我想到的是二十世纪二十年代的毕加索而不是伊万。）

感谢莎莉·金，我的编辑、朋友、我异父异母的妹妹、治疗师和咨询顾问。

感谢普特南出版社的团队：艾希礼·休利特（又名库尔特·安德尔森）、亚历克西斯·韦尔比、阿什利·麦克雷、布伦南·卡明斯和加布里埃拉·蒙盖利。

感谢《纽约客》杂志的苏珊·莫里森和艾玛·艾伦，

感谢她们最初在《纽约客》上刊登了我早期的诗作。

感谢值得信赖的读者和灵感提供者：苏兹·科克兰、金·加拉赫、迪伦·布鲁姆斯坦、利亚·马斯特罗贝蒂、亚历克山·英格兰德、里克·奈福、埃里克·卡尔森、像两岁孩子一样破口大骂的莱克斯·卡尔森、琳达·埃利亚尼和贝基·格雷。

感谢我的孩子们，露露和休伊特。

还有丽莎，我的妻子和我最好的朋友。在我们第三次约会时，我对她说："我不想要孩子。"谢天谢地，你没理会这句话。

ACKNOWLEDGMENTS

I would like to thank Kathy s., an Amazon.com reviewer of my previous book, *Love Poems for Married People*, who said, "This book is the worst." Also to the good people of the Russell Public Library, wherever that might be, who "HATED THIS BOOK SO MUCH" (their caps, not mine). They added, "It's crap." Thank you, Kathy and all of you at the Russell Public Library, for not believing in me. It was almost like being a kid again.

To Ivan Held, president of G. P. Putnam's Sons, who believed in *Love Poems for Married People* the moment it became a *New York Times* bestseller and who instantly greenlighted (-lit?) this book. As a result of the success of the first book, Ivan now lives in the South of France, where his paintings depict women with three boobs. (It's possible I'm thinking of Picasso in the 1920s and not Ivan.)

To Sally Kim, my editor, friend, sister-I-never-had, therapist, and guidance counselor.

To the team at G. P. Putnam's Sons. Ashley Hewlett (aka Kurt Andersen), Alexis Welby, Ashley McClay,

Brennin Cummings, and Gabriella Mongelli.

To Susan Morrison and Emma Allen at *The New Yorker* for running the earliest of these poems in the first place.

Trusted readers and idea generators: Suzi Corcoran, Kim Gallagher, Dylan Blumstein, Lea Mastroberti, Alexa Englander, Rick Knief, Eric Carlson, Lex Carlson for swearing as a two-year-old, Linda Elriani, and Becky Gray.

To my children, Lulu and Hewitt.

And to my wife and best friend, Lissa. To whom I said, on our third date, "I don't think I want children." Thank God you ignored me.